HUMAN BODY BOOK
INTRODUCTION TO THE MUSCULAR SYSTEM
Children's Anatomy & Physiology Edition

SPEEDY
PUBLISHING

Speedy Publishing LLC
40 E. Main St. #1156
Newark, DE 19711
www.speedypublishing.com

It takes 17 muscles in the face for us to smile and 43 muscles to frown.

The muscular
system is an organ
system consisting of
skeletal, smooth and
cardiac muscles.

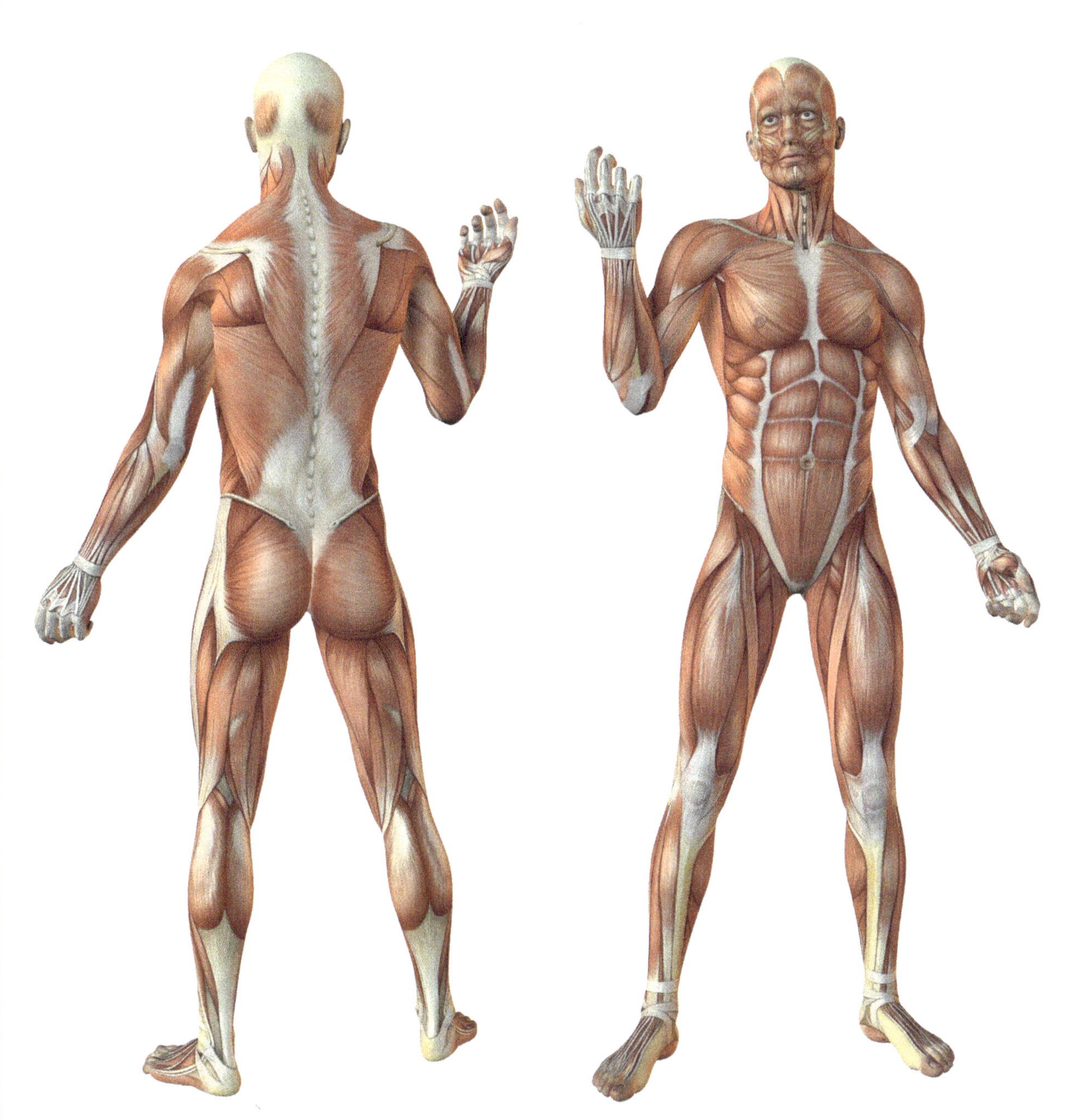

The muscular system
is responsible for
the movement of
the human body.

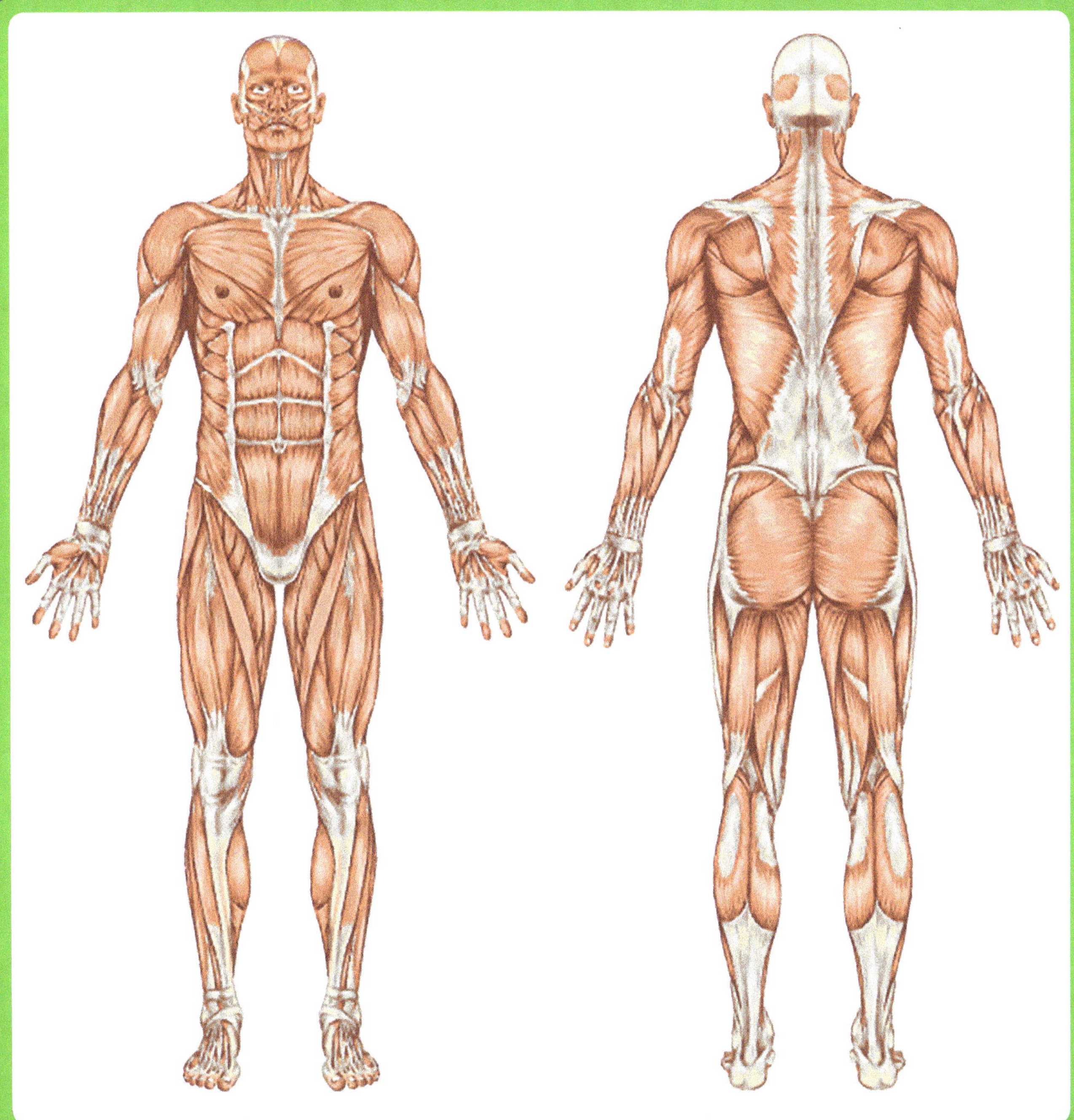

Some muscles work
without us thinking,
like our heart beating,
while other muscles
are controlled by
our thoughts and
allow us to do things
and move around.

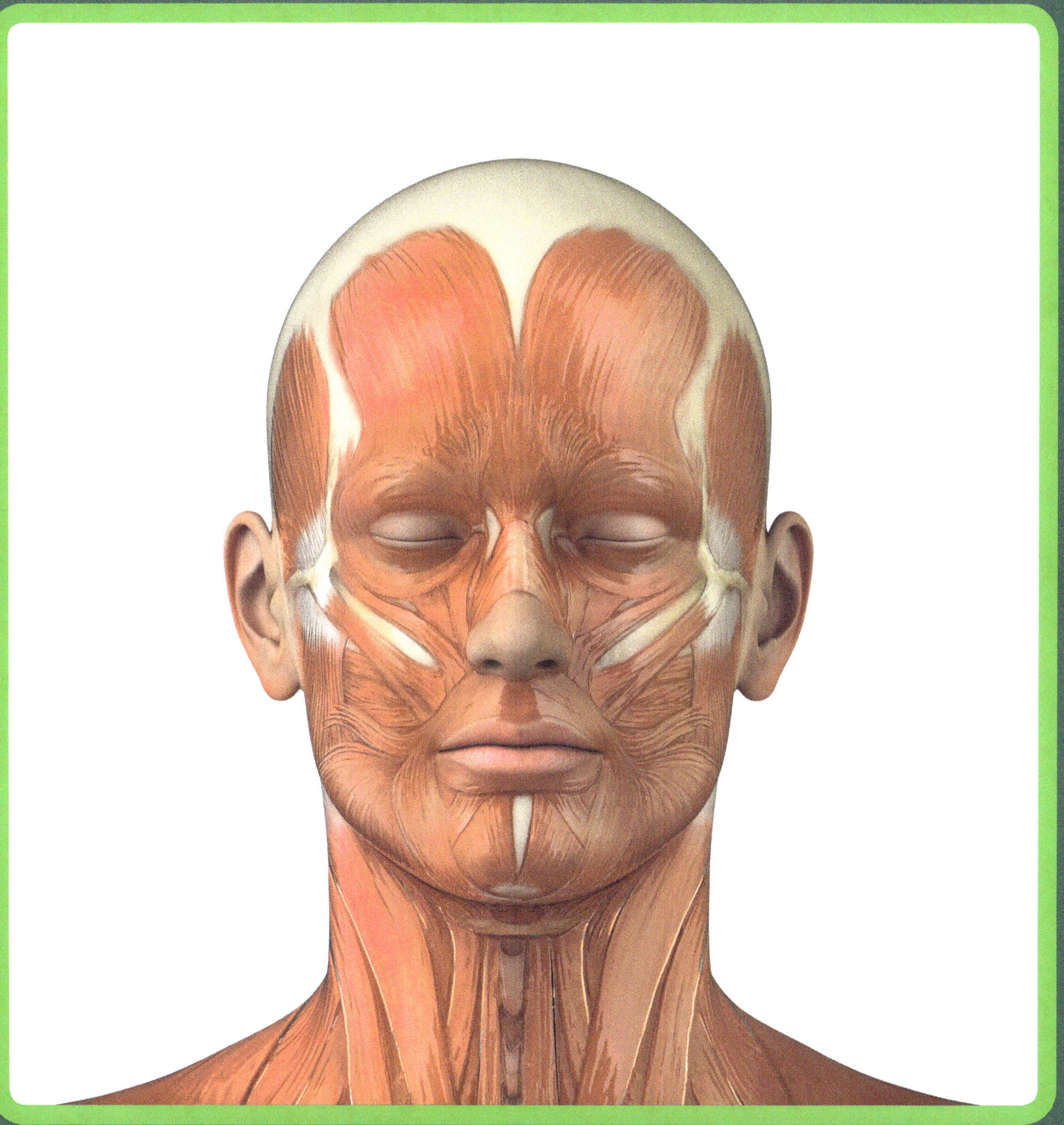

There are over
650 muscles in the
human body. Muscles
work by expanding
and contracting.

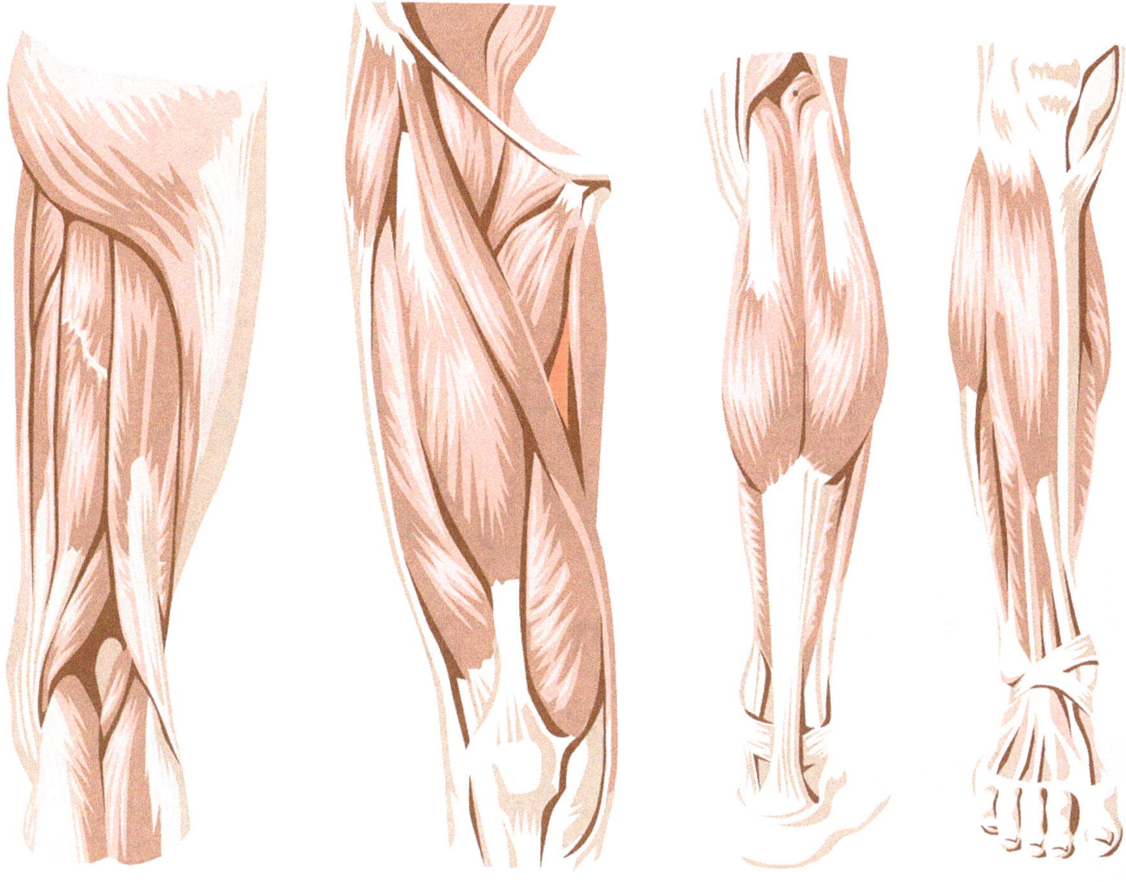

Muscles have long,
thin cells that are
grouped into bundles.

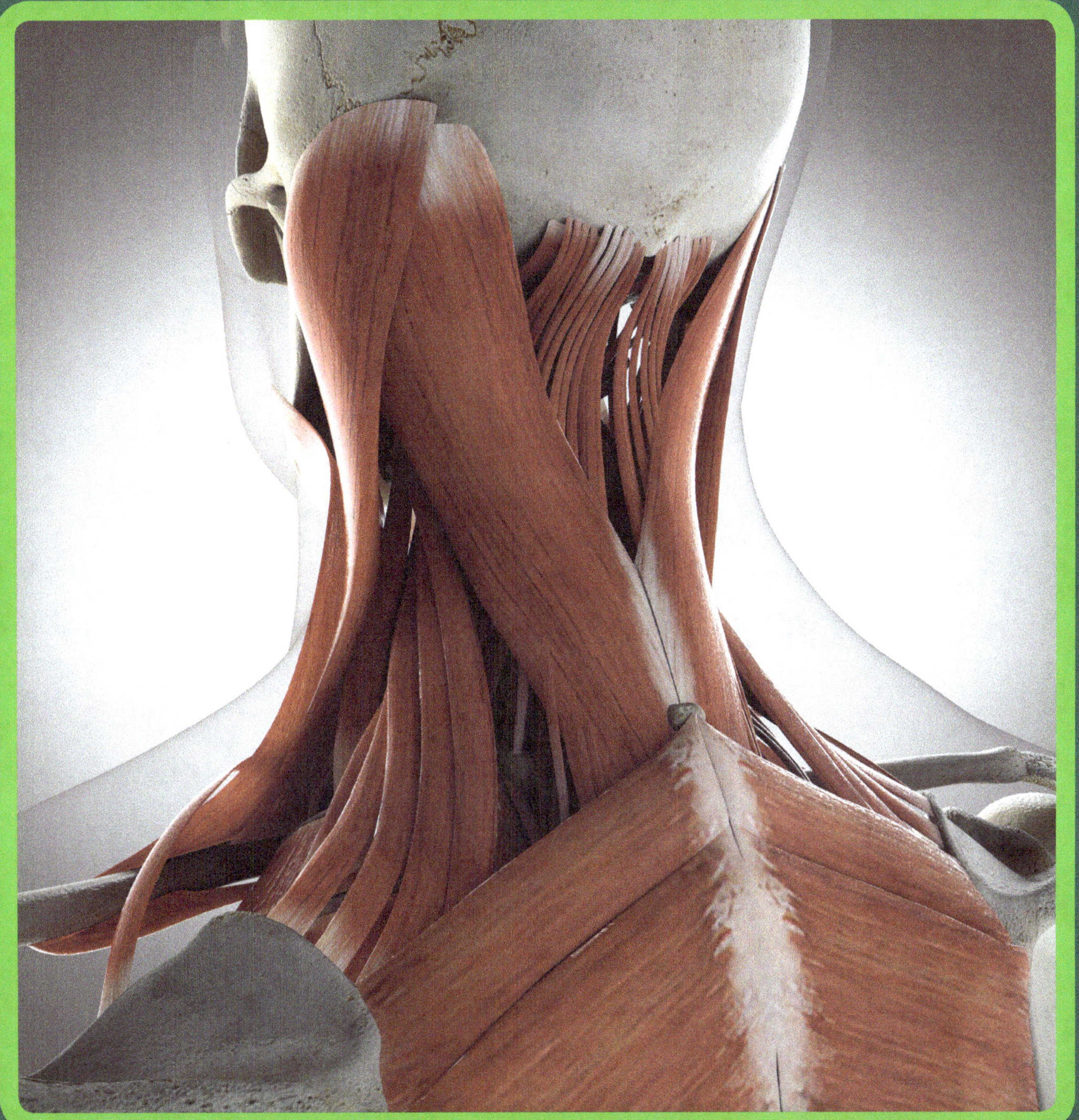

Many of our muscles come in pairs. Muscle pairs allow us to move back and forth.

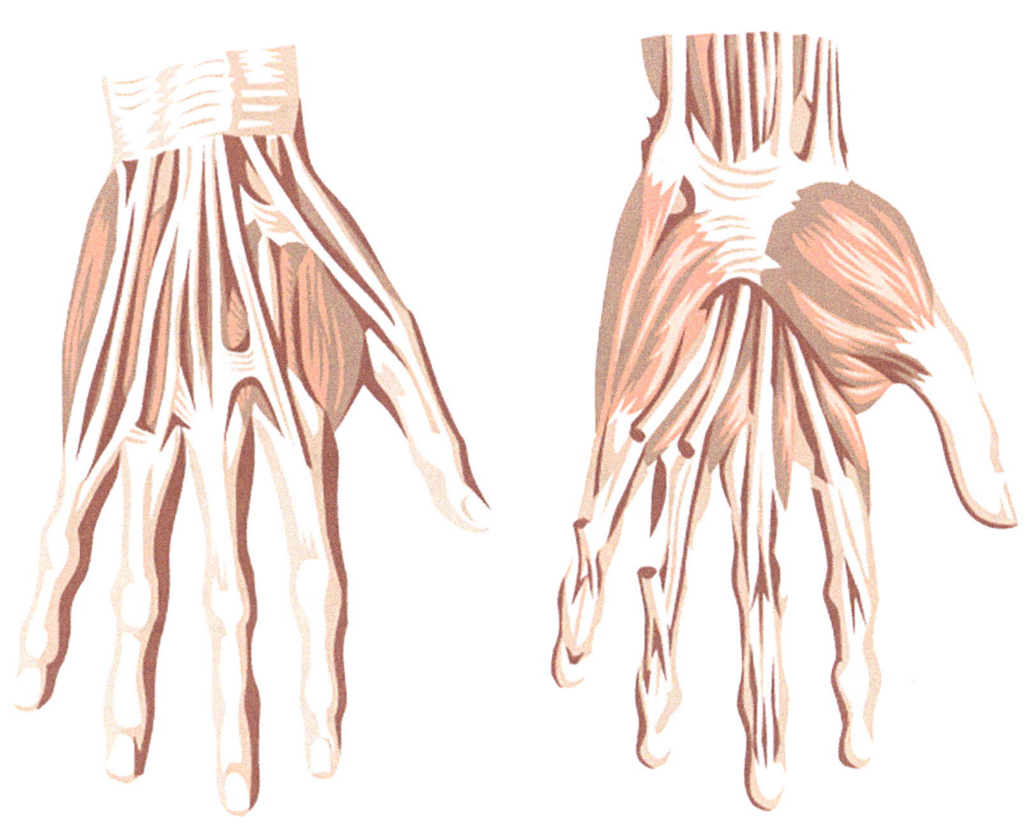

There are three distinct types of muscles: skeletal muscles, cardiac or heart muscles, and smooth muscles.

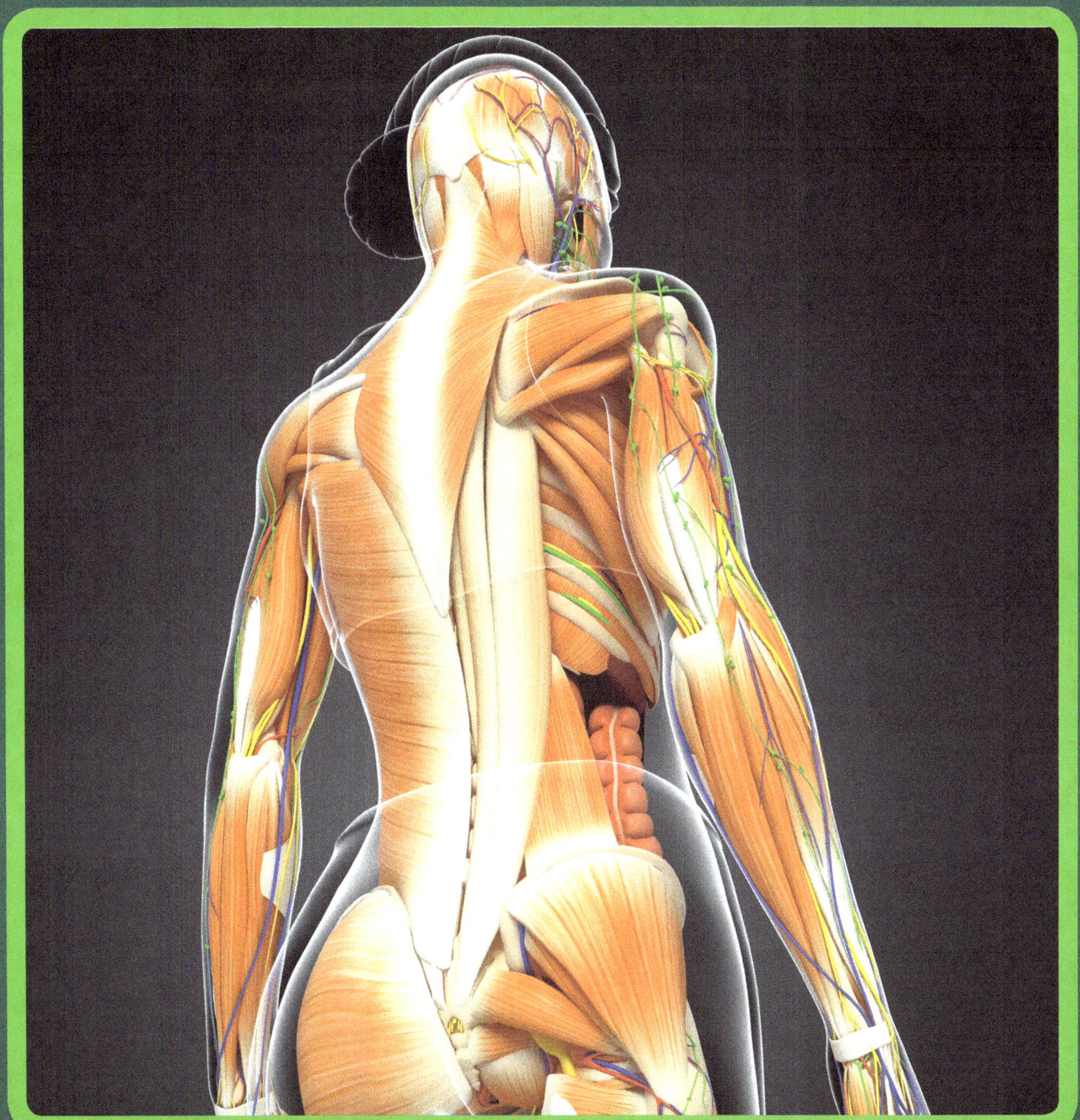

Cardiac muscle is also an involuntary muscle. It is only found in the heart.

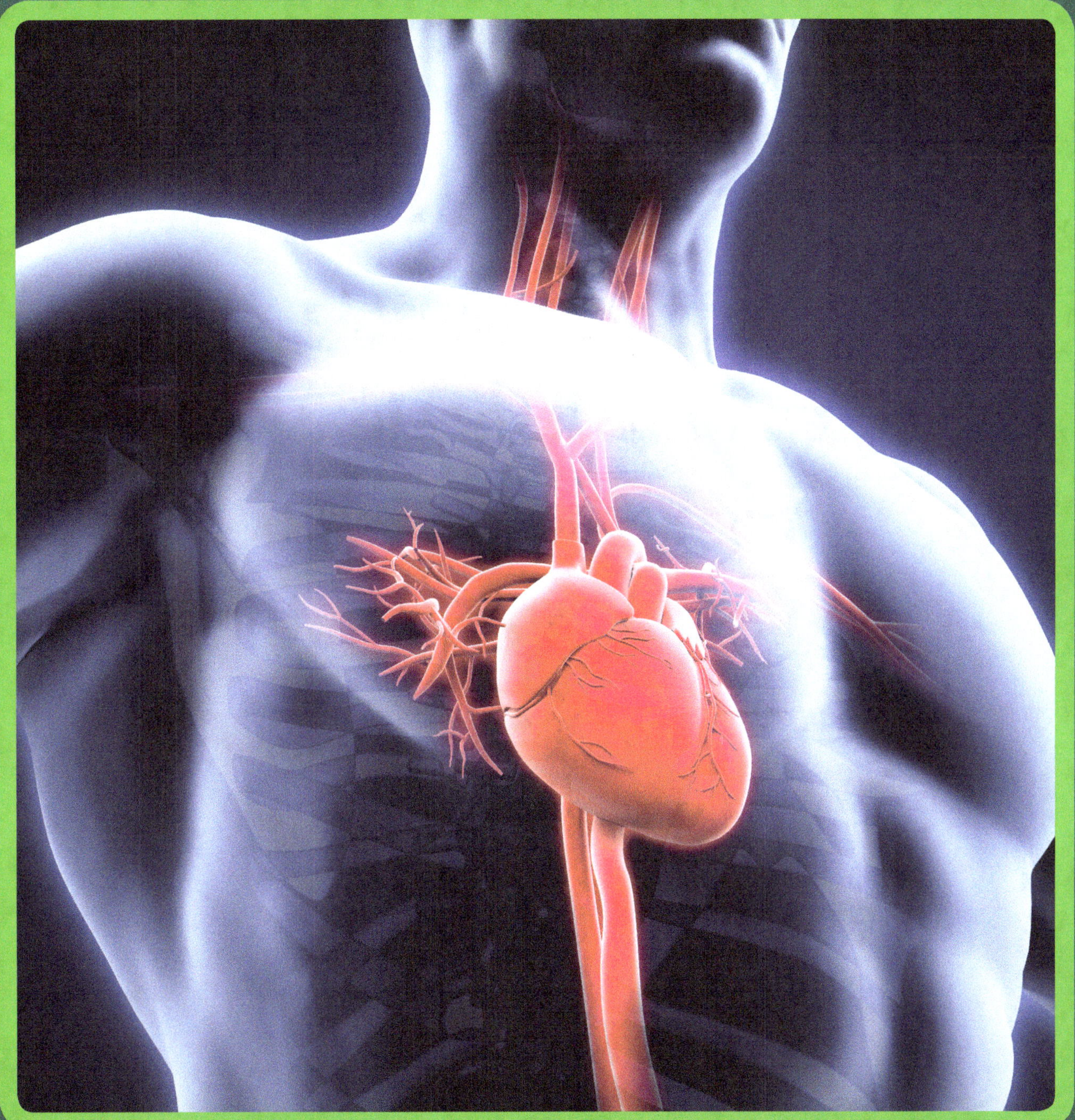

Cardiac muscle contracts tirelessly throughout life to pump blood from the heart to the lungs and around the body.

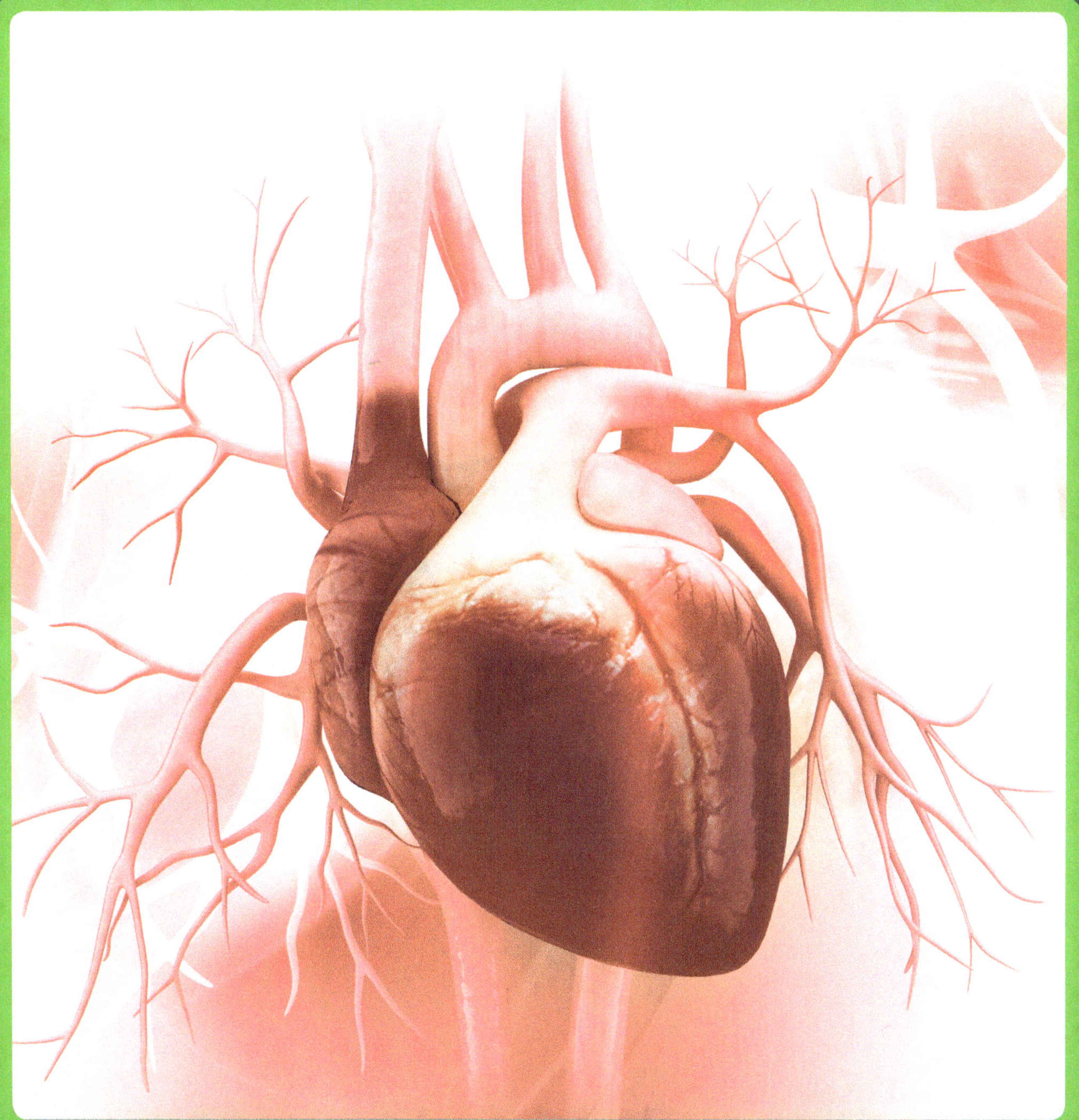

Skeletal muscles are
voluntary muscles
that control nearly
every action a person
intentionally performs.

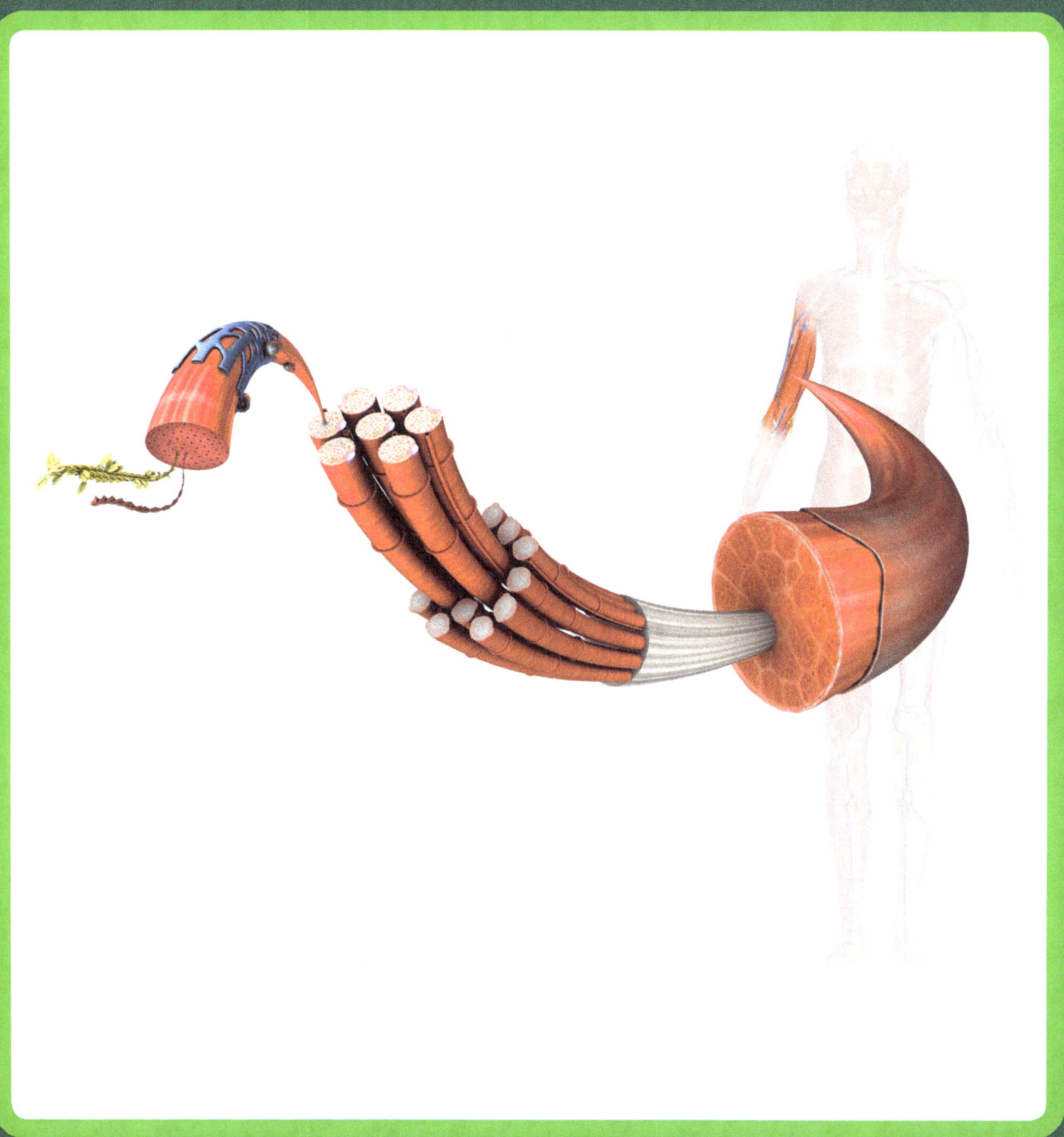

They cover our skeleton and move our bones. There are approximately 639 skeletal muscles in the human body.

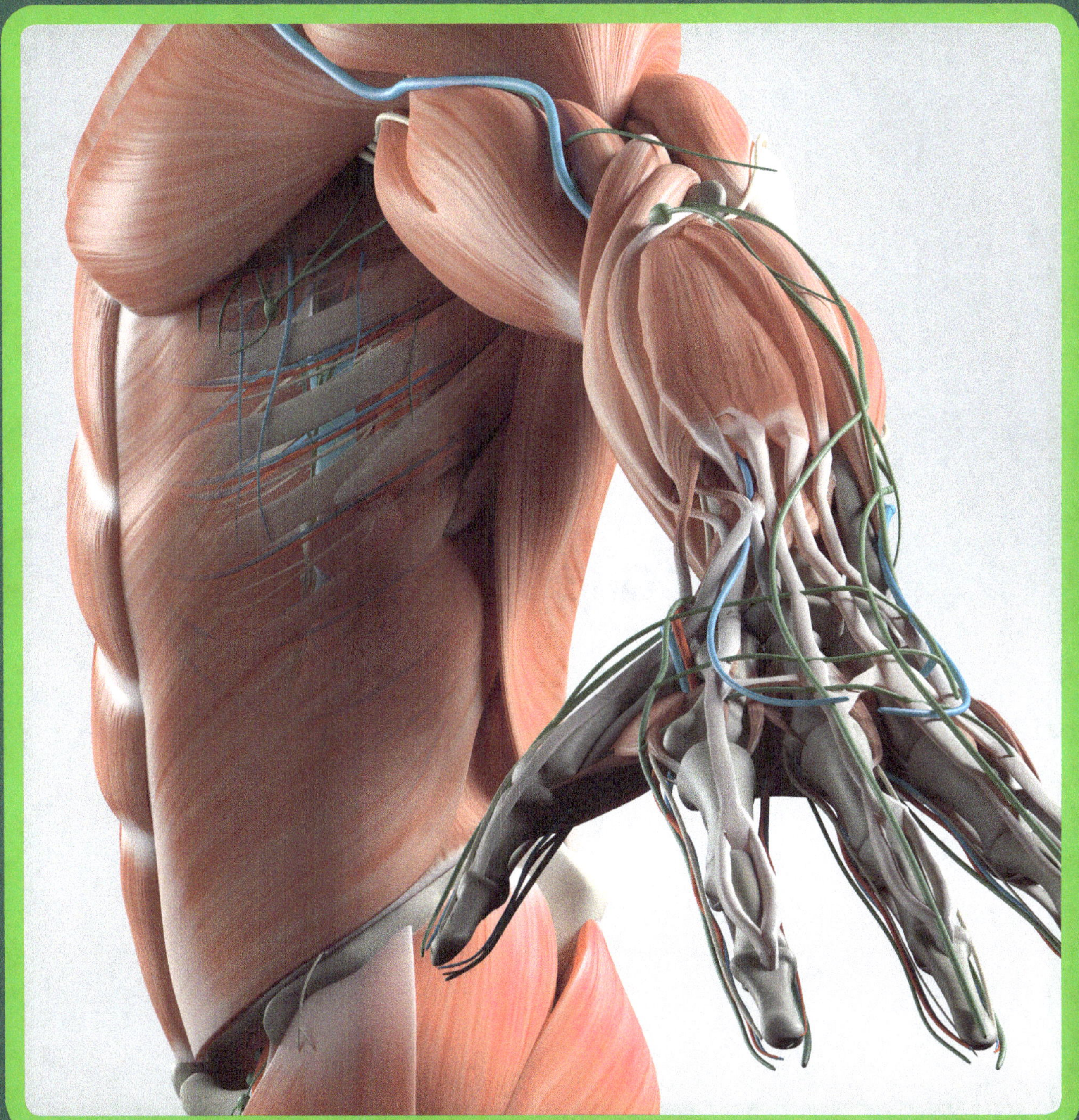

Skeletal muscle is
also called striated
or striped muscle.

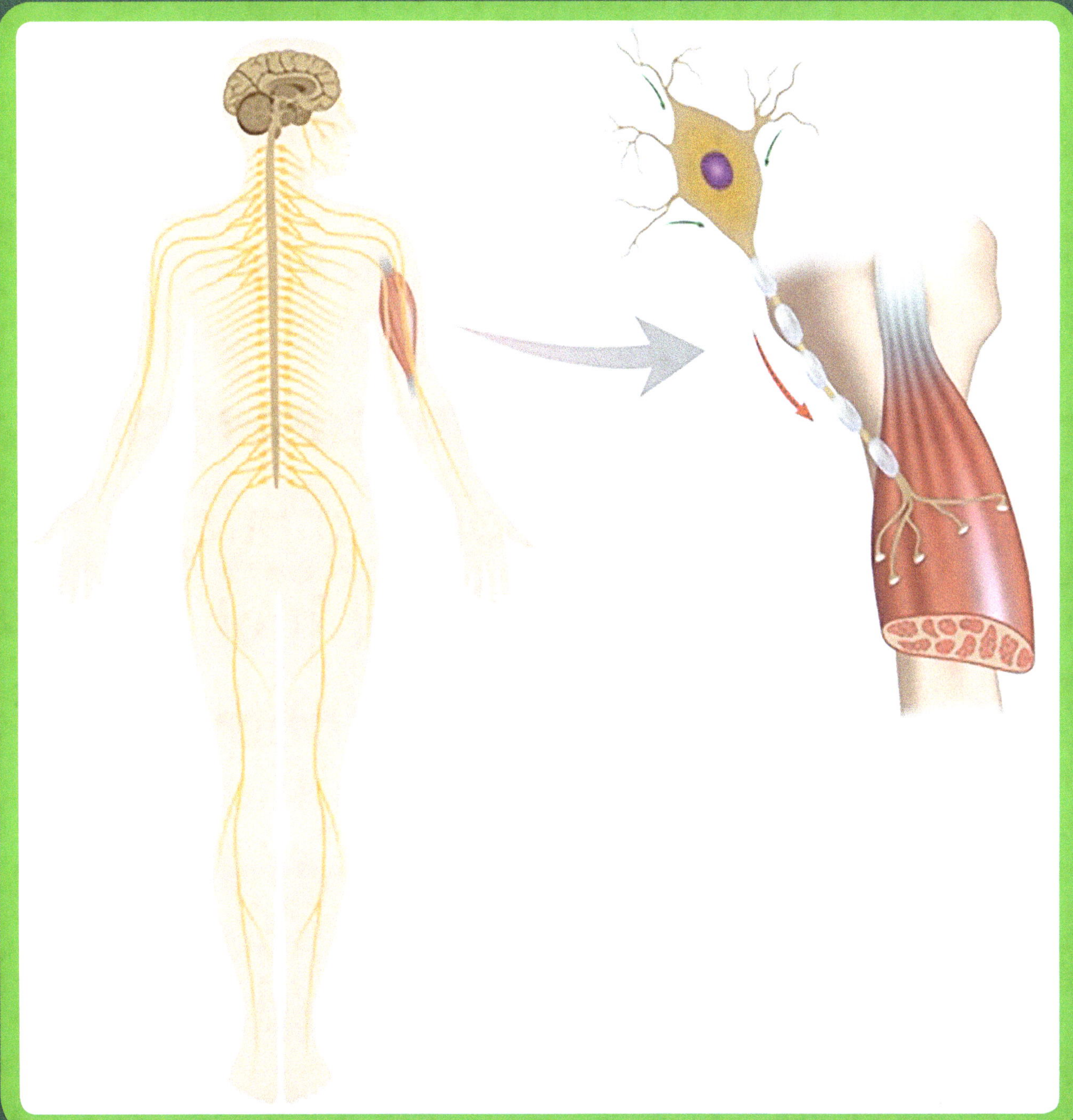

Smooth muscles are special muscles that don't connect to bones, but control organs within our body.

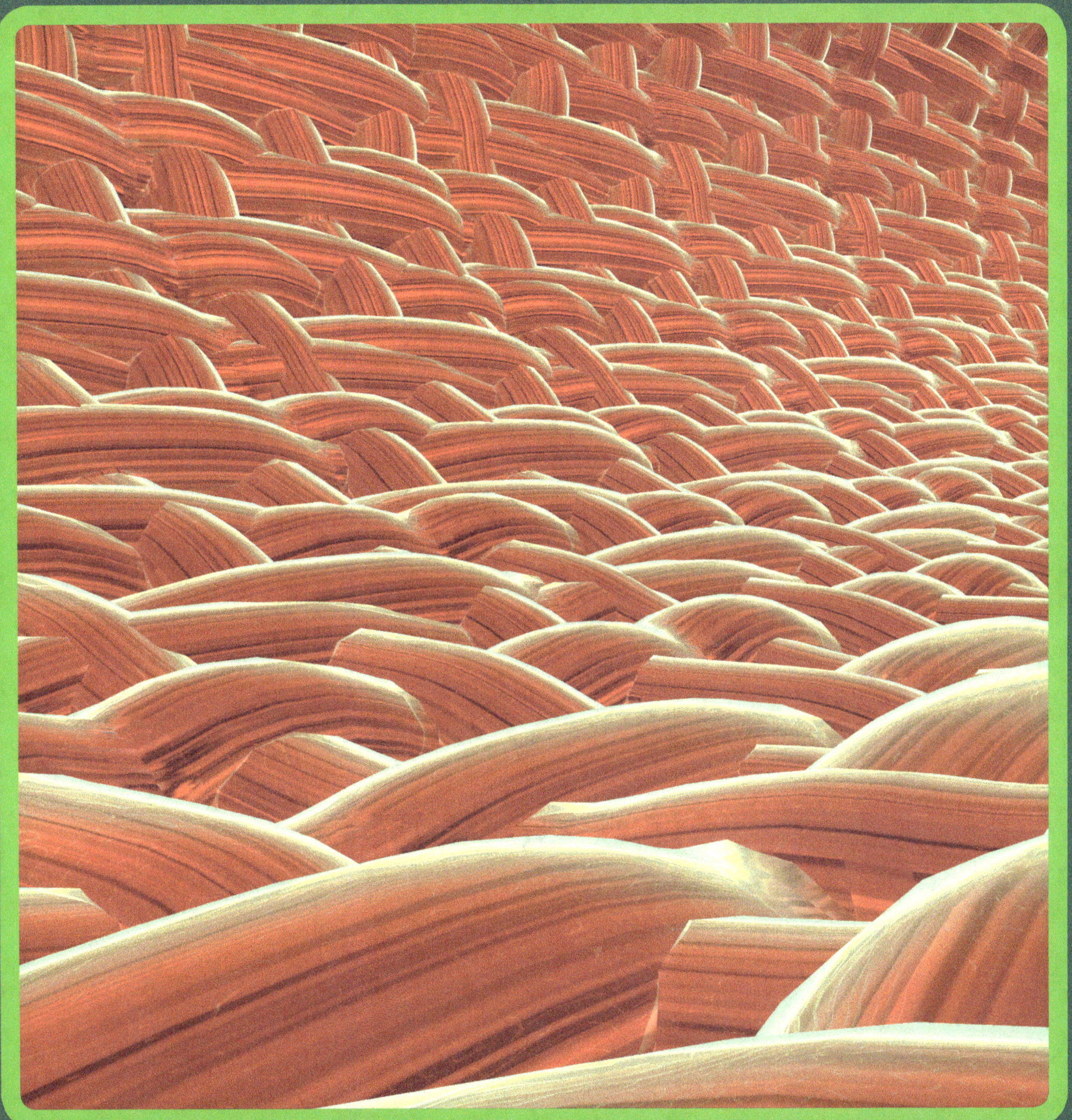

Smooth muscle is involuntary. Smooth muscles contract to move substances such as food through the organ.

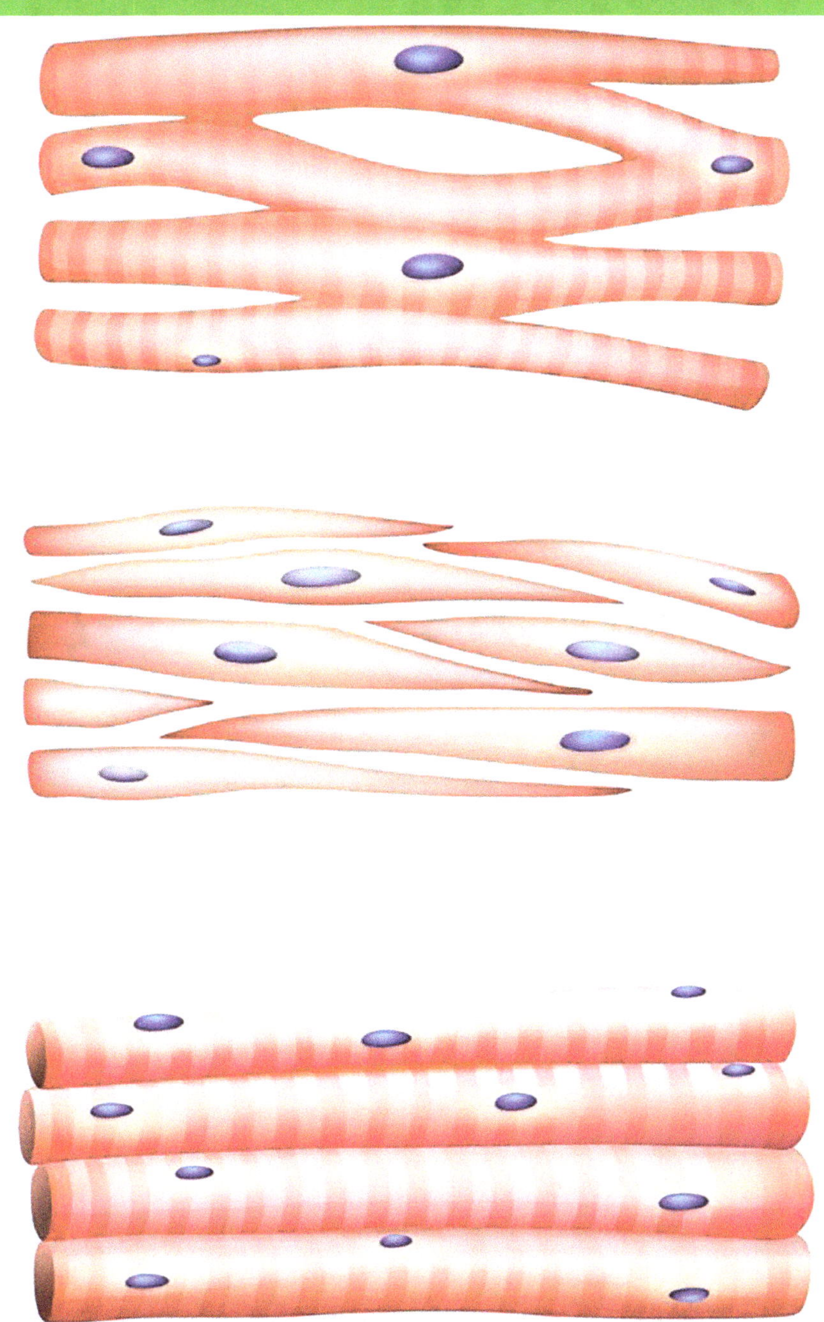

Muscles make up 40% of your total body weight.

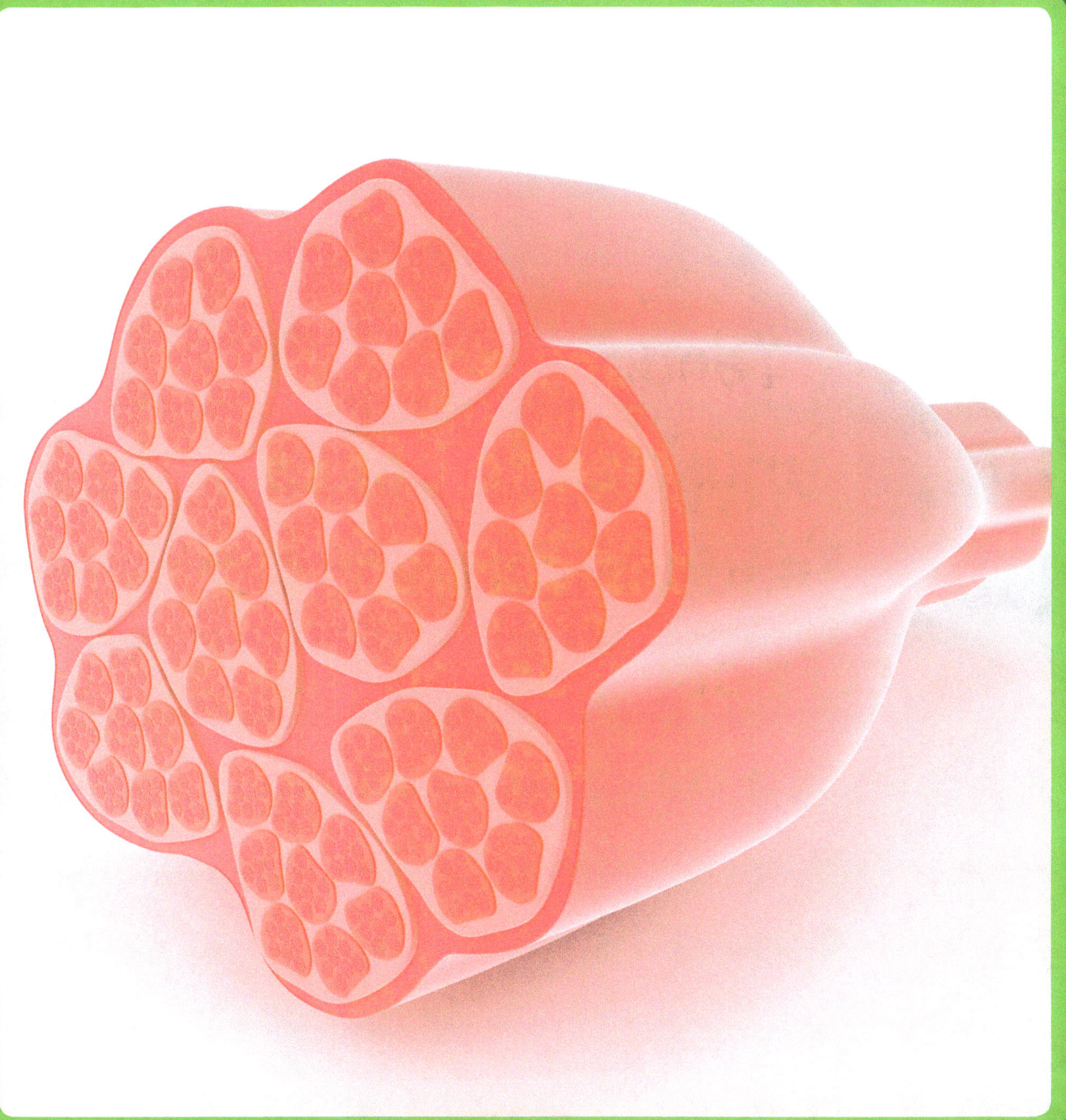

Tendons connect muscles to bones. Tendons connect our soft contracting muscle to our hard bones.

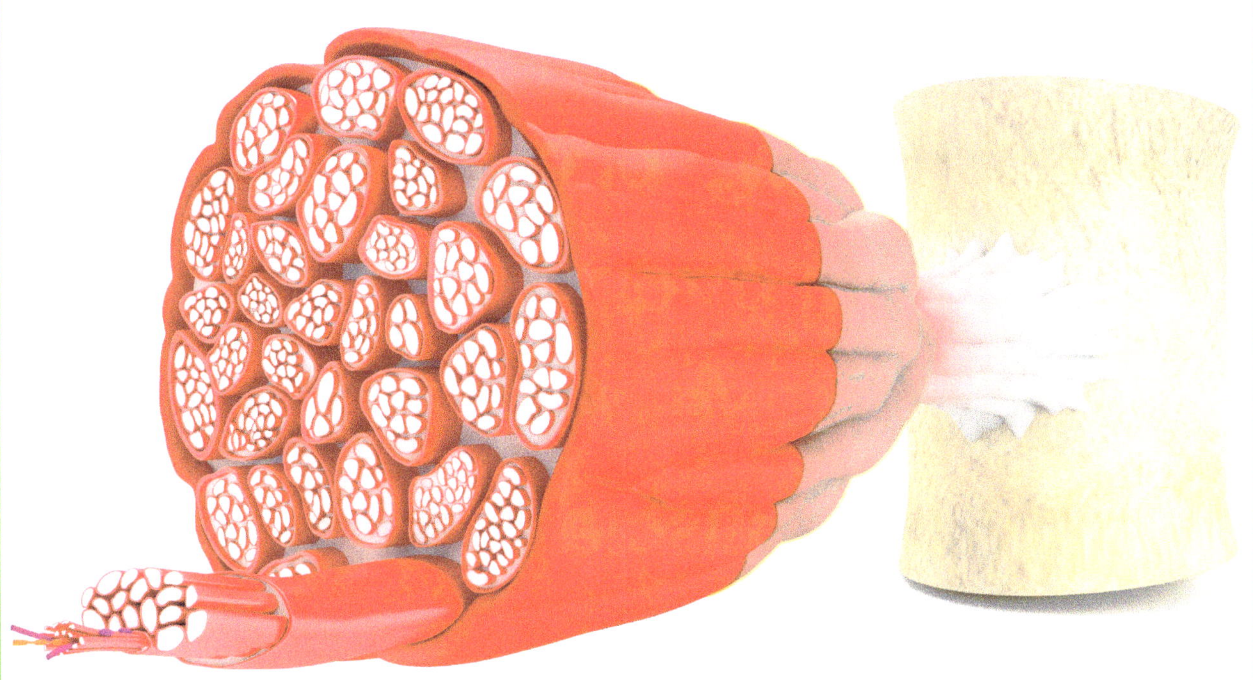

When we practice an action over and over again, we get what is called muscle memory.

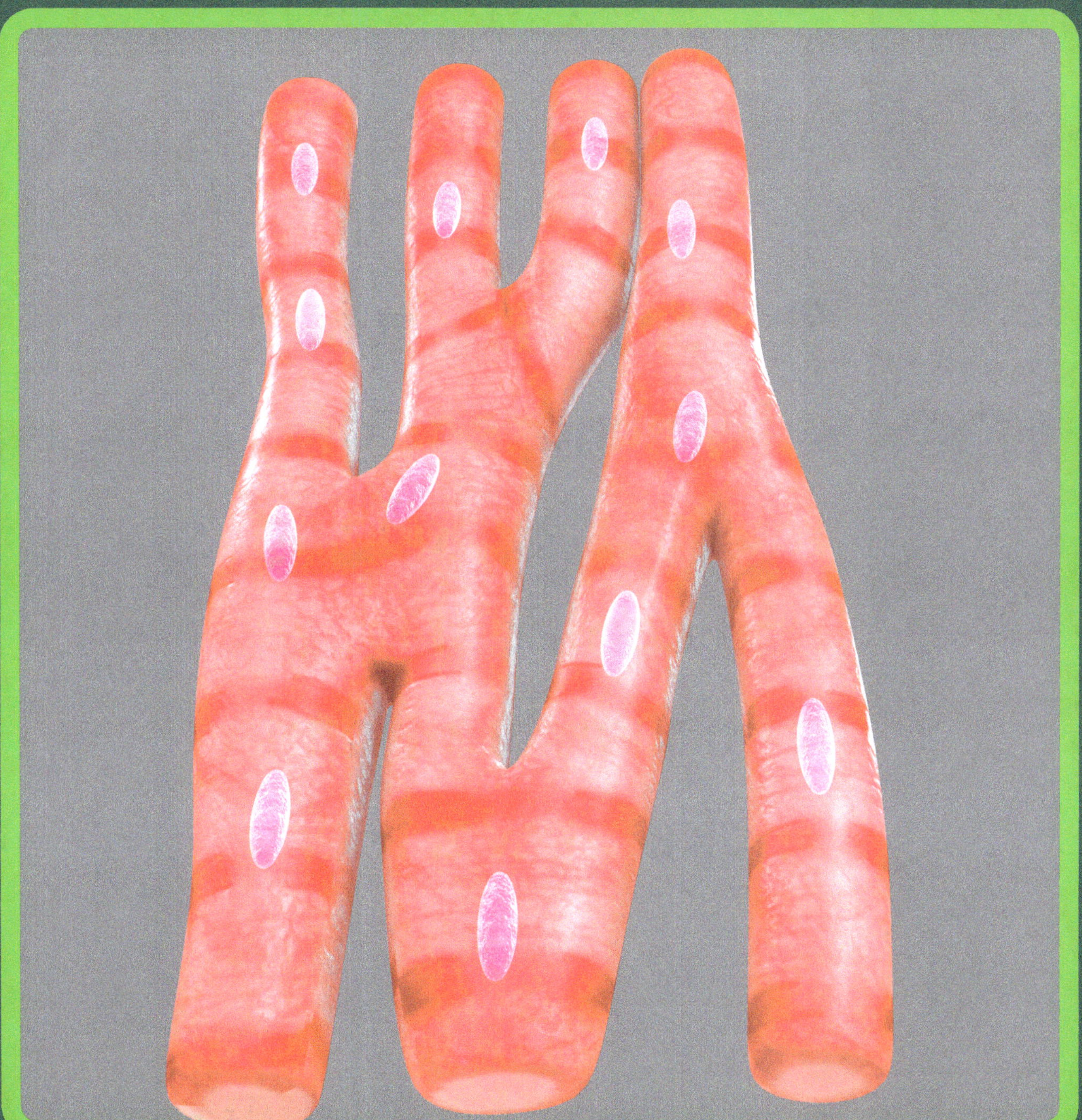

Shivering is caused
by hundreds of
muscles expanding
and contracting to
produce heat and
make us warmer.

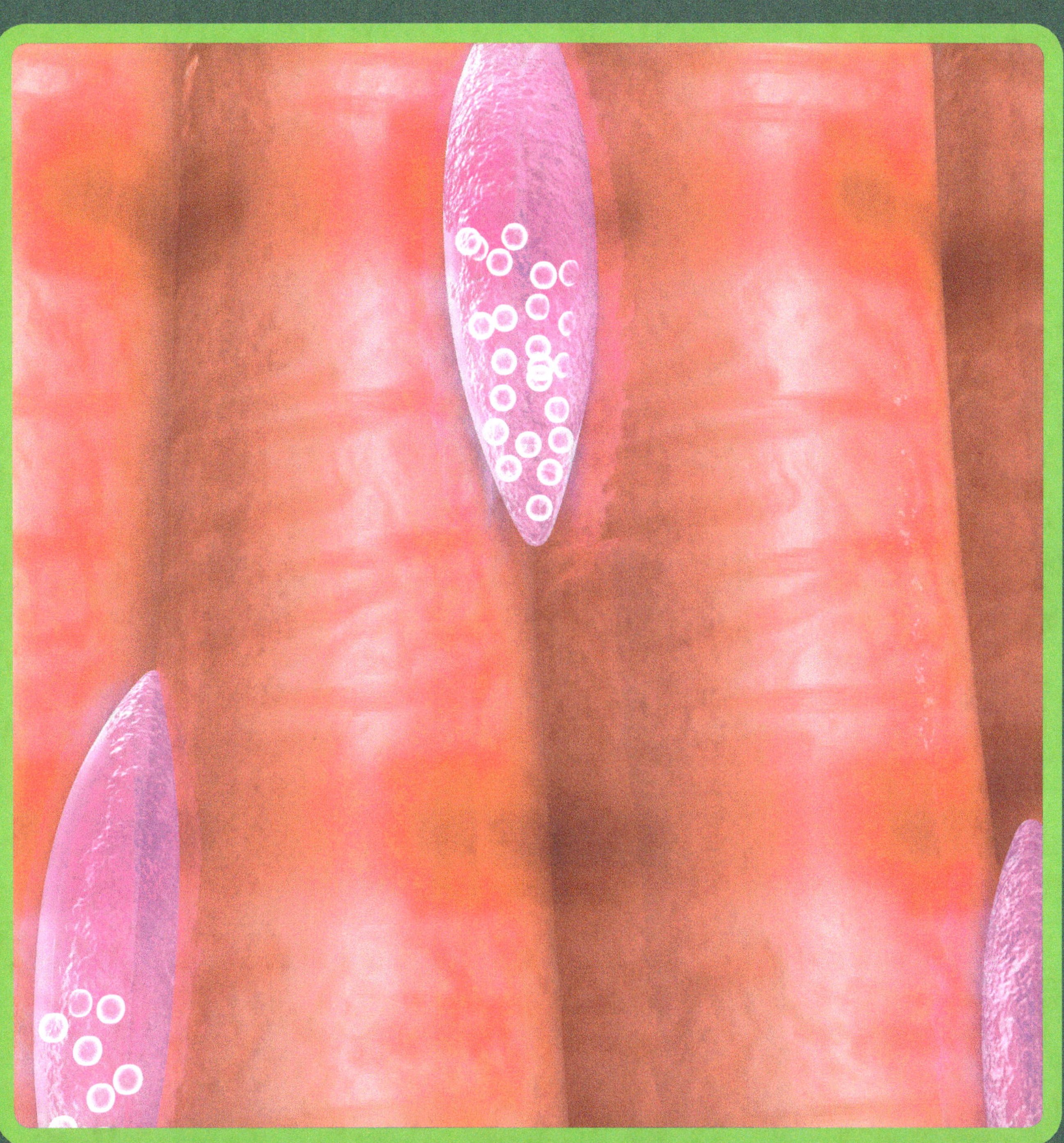

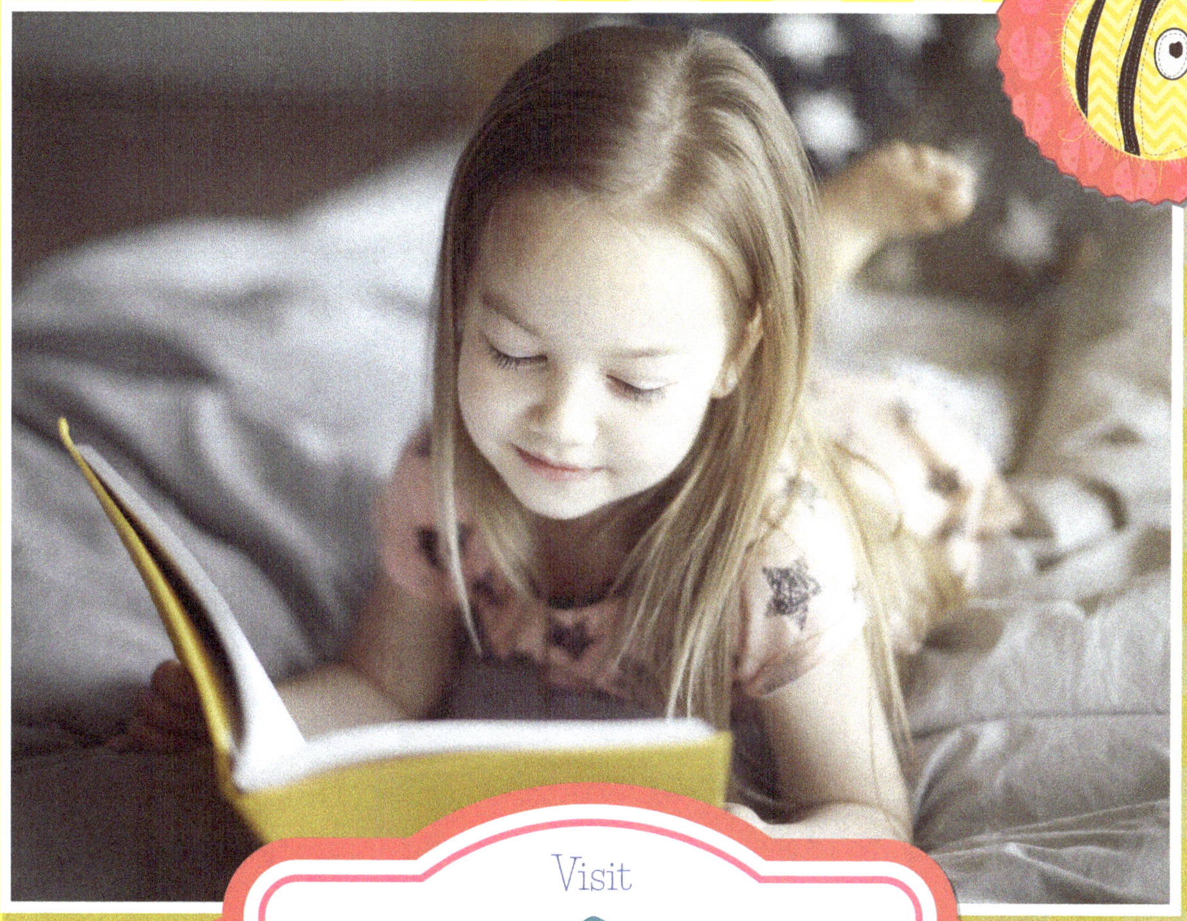

Visit

BABY PROFESSOR
EDUCATION KIDS

www.BabyProfessorBooks.com

to download Free Baby Professor eBooks and view our catalog of new and exciting Children's Books